THIS BOOK BELONGS TO

. . . .

. . . .

To Noah and Gabriel with love – T.K.

To my darling girls Tils, Bea and Martha xxx – J.B.

First published 2022 by Macmillan Children's Books
an imprint of Pan Macmillan
The Smithson, 6 Briset Street, London EC1M 5NR
EU representative: Macmillan Publishers Ireland Limited,
1st Floor, The Liffey Trust Centre, 117-126 Sheriff Street Upper,
Dublin 1, D01 YC43
Associated companies throughout the world
www.panmacmillan.com

Hardback ISBN: 978-1-5098-4859-1
Paperback ISBN: 978-1-5098-4860-7

Text copyright © Timothy Knapman 2022
Illustrations copyright © Joe Berger 2022

Moral rights asserted.

The right of Timothy Knapman and Joe Berger to be identified as the
author and illustrator of this work has been asserted by them in
accordance with the Copyright, Designs and Patents Act 1988.

1 3 5 7 9 8 6 4 2

A CIP catalogue record for this book is available from the British Library.

Printed in Spain

SOMETIMES I JUST
WON'T

TIMOTHY KNAPMAN

JOE BERGER

MACMILLAN CHILDREN'S BOOKS

Sometimes I am helpful –
look at me, I'm good as gold.

Sometimes I will smile and
do exactly what I'm told.

And sometimes I just won't.

Sometimes I will wait my turn
and try the tallest slide.

Sometimes
I'll put on my coat
when it is cold outside.

And **SOMETIMES**

I just won't.

Sometimes I'll eat everything and say,
"That's yum! More please!"

SO SOMETIMES

I JUST WON'T.

And when Dad says, "It's getting late.
High time you were in bed."

I DON'T CARE if I'm really tired,
I'll go downstairs instead!

I don't want to stroke the doggies!
They might do something bad.

But then I see how sweet they are,
and really wish I had.

So now I don't know
what I want.

Except I don't want this . . .

And that's when someone picks me up
and calms me with a kiss.

She tells me that she understands,
that I *should* get to choose.
If something isn't feeling right,
it's OK to refuse.

But sometimes things look scary,
when actually they're fun.

And you won't know you like them,
until they're halfway done.

So now I'm **BRAVE** and try new things
I've never tried before.

I share,

I help,

I eat **ALL** food –
I even ask for more!

Though most things make me happy,

there are still a few that **DON'T**.

But I don't let them bother me
because sometimes . . .